MACHINE MANIA

SUPERCARS

Frances Ridley

Copyright © ticktock Entertainment Ltd 2007
First published in Great Britain in 2007 by ticktock Media Ltd.,
Unit 2, Orchard Business Centre, North Farm Road,
Tunbridge Wells, Kent, TN2 3XF

ticktock project editor: Julia Adams
ticktock project designer: Emma Randall

We would like to thank: Alix Wood.

ISBN 978 1 84696 561 6

Printed in China
9 8 7 6 5 4 3 2

Picture credits
b=bottom; c=centre; t=top; r=right; l=left
All images Car Photo Library-www.carphoto.co.uk, except: Alamy: 3b, 4-5c, 5tr, 20-21c;
Auto Express: 8-9c, 9tr; www.bugatti-cars.de: 21tr

Every effort has been made to trace the copyright holders,
and we apologise in advance for any unintentional omissions.
We would be pleased to insert the appropriate acknowledgements
in any subsequent edition of this publication.

Contents

Lamborghini Murcielago

The Murcielago's **engine** is behind the driver's seat. It has a top speed of 330 km/h.

This Murcielago's doors open from the roof. When they open they look like a seagull's wings. They are called gull-wing doors.

Bugatti EB110

Ettore Bugatti started the Bugatti company. The EB110 was named after him.

The car's **body** is made of **carbon fibre**. This makes it very light. Its **dashboard** is made of wood, like an old-fashioned sports car!

The EB110 has a top speed of 336 km/h. It can **accelerate** from 0 to 100 km/h in 3.2 seconds!

Noble M15

This **supercar** has a twin-turbo **engine**. It can **accelerate** from 0 to 97 km/h in 3.3 seconds.

The Noble M15 has a top speed of 297 km/h. It also has satellite navigation. This means the driver will never get lost!

The Noble M15 was made for everyday use. It has soft leather seats and 300 litres of luggage space.

Chrysler Viper GTS

The Viper GTS was designed by Caroll Shelby. He also designed American racing cars.

The Viper GTS replaced the Dodge Viper. The Dodge Viper only came in red or yellow. The Viper GTS comes in lots of colours, but all the cars have stripes!

The Viper GTS has an enormous V10 **engine**. This kind of engine was designed for trucks!

Ferrari F50

Ferrari is famous for its sports cars. By 1996, it had made sports cars for 50 years. It launched a special car to celebrate. The car was called the F50!

The F50's **engine** is nearly as powerful as a **Formula One** engine. The exhausts stick out of holes in the back, just like a racing car! Its top speed is 325 km/h.

Jaguar XJ220S

The XJ220S was based on a **Le Mans** racing car. The XJ220S has a **carbon fibre body**. This makes it very light.

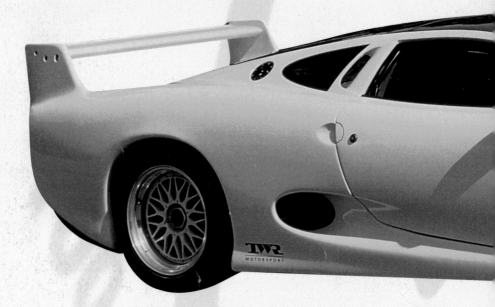

The XJ220S was the fastest road car of its time. Its top speed is 349 km/h.

It is very wide for a sports car. It has a huge wing at the back.

McLaren F1

McLaren are famous for making **Formula One** racing cars. They wanted to make the best **supercar** in the world.

The F1 was the fastest road car of its time. It is still one of the most famous cars in the world. Its top speed is 386 km/h.

The F1 was very expensive. It cost £634,500. Each F1 car took nearly two months to make. McLaren only made 100 F1s.

Pagani Zonda C12 S

The Pagani Zonda was launched in 2001. Its top speed is 354 km/h. It was designed by Horacio Pagani. 'Zonda' is the name of a fast wind.

The Pagani Zonda looks like a fighter plane. It has a glass roof and an exhaust like a rocket.

It has a huge **engine** made by AMG. They also make racing car engines for Mercedes-Benz.

Bugatti Veyron

The Bugatti Veyron has a top speed of 407 km/h. Only 70 have been made.

It can **accelerate** from 0 to 100 km/h in 2.5 seconds!

The Veyron is the most expensive **production car** in the world. Each one costs £840,000.

TVR Tuscan

The TVR Tuscan was launched in 2000. It's very light and has a huge **engine**. The Tuscan's top speed is 290 km/h.

You can take the Tuscan's roof off. It fits inside the large boot.

The Tuscan doesn't have door handles. You press a button under the wing mirror to get in. You twist a knob inside the car to get out!

GDB 341

Glossary

Accelerate   To get faster.

Body   The part of the car that covers the frame and engine.

Carbon fibre   A light material used to make cars strong.

Dashboard   The panel behind the steering wheel that has a speedometer and other dials.

Engine   The part of the car where fuel is burned to make energy.

Formula One   A famous series of motor races.

Le Mans   A famous race in France – it takes place in the town of Le Mans.

Production car   A car not designed only for racing.

Supercar   A very fast, expensive car.